Planning for Awesome

7 Steps to Ensure Your Strategic Planning Session Turns out Amazing

Todd R. Christensen

Dedication

For my father, Theodore Christensen, and his example of dedication to and love for his business and, more importantly, his patients.

For my mother, Nola Myrl Christensen, for her own dedication and contributions to the business of family.

Planning for Awesome: 7 Steps to Ensure Your Strategic Planning Session Turns out Amazing

Copyright © 2019 by Todd R. Christensen, TAWC Enterprises llc

All rights reserved. No part of this book may be reproduced or transmitted in any form or by any means without written permission from the author.

Printed in USA by TAWC Enterprises llc, Meridian, Idaho (208-649-4788)

Table of Contents

Chapter One: Introduction 11

Chapter Two: What Strategy DOES for Your 13

    Stress Less Strategies Decrease, well, Stress 13

    Stress Less Strategies Decrease Busywork 14

    Stress Less Strategies Provide a Compass for Adrift Organizations 15

    Stress Less Strategies Provide Confidence for Organizational Leaders 15

    Stress Less Strategies Boost Fundraising 15

    Stress Less Strategies Lift Employee Engagement 16

    Stress Less Strategies Add New Life to Workplace Doldrums 16

    Stress Less Strategies Encourage Employee and Leadership Accountability 17

Chapter Three: The Strategic Planning Session 19

    Step 1: Location, Location, Location 19

    Step 2: Choose an Independent, Experienced and Unbiased Facilitator 21

    Step 3: Inviting the Right Stakeholders 22

    Step 4: Setting the Date 24

    Step 5: Creating the Agendas 25

    Step 6: Supplies & Equipment 27

    Step 7: The Set Up 27

Chapter Four: Conclusion 29

Glossary 31

Index 33

About the Author 35

Chapter One: Introduction

For many years, the word "Strategy" conjured up visions in my mind of great military leaders surveying battlefields full of armies engaged in desperate struggles. I saw business leadership teams huddled over maps and around chalk boards diagramming successful campaigns.

Unfortunately, I had it all wrong. What I was thinking of when I heard the term, "strategy," was actually more related to tactics. Tactics are plans for achieving short-term goals, such as winning a battle or creating a winning marketing campaign. Perhaps I can blame it on my childhood experiences with the game, "Stratego," that associates the word, "strategy," with a 25-minute board game. Chess and the game, Risk, on the other hand, have much more to do with strategy. Both acknowledge the fact that you can win a battle but lose the war.

Tactics are short-term. Strategy is long-term. Tactics are what you want to DO. Strategy is what you want to ACHIEVE.

If strategy sounds overwhelming or, in the immortal words of *the Princess Bride*'s Vizzini, "Inconceivable," then this booklet is for you.

Too many nonprofit leaders stress about the thought of holding a strategic planning session. They worry about "getting it right." They fear "missing something." So they don't even start. Strategic planning should not be stressful. In fact, it should be something anticipated each year or two and revisited regularly in between.

Whether you have an established strategic plan or whether you are thinking about holding your first strategic planning session, you will find in this booklet various practical guides and tools.

Let's get going!

Chapter Two: What Strategy DOES for Your Organization

If you are reading this booklet, the thought of creating a strategy for your business, your nonprofit, you association, your club or your organization likely creates fear in your heart or trepidation in your mind. You may worry that you are not up to the task or that your team will resent the requirement to attend. Whatever the reason you have for attempting to create a strategy, you must first find a good reason to do so.

Stress Less Strategies Decrease, well, Stress

One of the best reasons to develop a strategy for your organization is to actually decrease stress upon your leadership (board, management, executive director) and employees. Strategy takes the guess work out of determining whether an activity or an effort and a program is appropriate and acceptable. It answers the question that should be on all employees' minds: "Is this the best use of my time?"

Stress is the uncomfortable difference created when expectation does not match reality.

Strategy creates the framework of reality around which all efforts should be built.

Strategy gives all involved a purposeful approach to their work and turns even failures into meaningfulness.

All employees and all programs fail at one point or another. If we have a strategy in place, failure can serve as a learning experience rather than a death sentence.

Strategy is not a day-to-day project. Strategy is a long-term hope.

Strategy is not a goal to achieve this year. It is the identified plan and the artful approach by which we achieve ultimate success.

Strategy is not the same as your mission statement. The mission statement is the acknowledged purpose for your organization's existence. Strategy is the identification of the ultimate approach you will take to make your mission a reality.

General Grant, during the U.S. Civil War, identified his winning strategy long before he took control of the Union

Army. He knew that the South did not have the capability to sustain long-term war if their access to waterways in the West (the Mississippi), their agricultural production, and their railways ceased to exist. His strategy was not to win battles. Winning battles involved tactics. Winning battles achieved temporary success and even fame (as is still the case for the great Confederate tactician, General, Robert E. Lee). Grant knew that to achieve his mission of winning the war, he needed to destroy the South's ability to wage it. He created an overall plan of what would ultimately lead to the achievement of his mission. This approach to cutting off the South from their western waterways, destroying their agricultural production centers, and disrupting their rail transport systems made up his strategy.

Too often we focus our efforts on winning battles. We set daily, weekly, monthly and even annual goals that we can celebrate with or crow about to our funders, board members and supporters on websites, in annual reports, and on posters in front offices. But at the end of the day or week or month or year, even after winning these short-term battles, we may be no closer to winning the war for our mission if they are not intricately tied to an overall strategy of achieving our mission. Otherwise, they become Potemkin Villages. They create the illusion we are doing a lot of work, but they hide the reality that it is mostly busywork.

Stress Less Strategies Decrease Busywork

Speaking of busywork, nonprofit executive directors and presidents who are constantly overworked, approaching burn out, and struggling to keep their head above water are those most likely not to have a strategic plan in place. There is much to do to achieve success, but strategic plans not only identify the path to success, they clearly delineate assignments and accountability.

For those organizations whose funding is not yet sufficient to hire additional staff to take the current burden off the executive director, a strategic plan illuminates the stairway, step-by-step, to such points, allowing leadership to put aside the less important tasks and focus on priorities.

Strategic plans will save the overworked executive on the verge of burn out

Overburdened nonprofit leaders are most in need of strategic plans.

Stress Less Strategies Provide a Compass for Adrift Organizations

Whether in start up mode or long-established, executive directors and boards of many nonprofits find themselves feeling adrift after a few months or years. They may have a mission statement, but they seem to be treading water, going through the motions or just stuck in daily routines. It seems that no matter how busy they are, nothing seems to make a difference.

Enter strategy. Strategic planning is the compass, the map and the trail guide such organizations. Strategy provides purpose, identifies the reasons for which leaders and employees show up to work, and creates the tools that all involved will use to move from point A to point B.

Strategy is not only the sail for the organizational ship. Strategy provides the wind and even the direction from which it blows.

Stress Less Strategies Provide Confidence for Organizational Leaders

Having a strategic plan in place is a confidence booster for all leadership involved, from the board to the executives to the managers. Not only does it serve as a roadmap when leadership is feeling at a loss on what to do throughout the year, it can serve as the basis for onboarding new leadership.

Without a strategic plan, not only are you a driver in the wilderness without a map or a compass, but you are without an understanding of where you even want to go.

Stress Less Strategies Boost Fundraising

Having a compelling mission statement is critically important to nonprofit fundraising. Foundations, individual donors and philanthropic organizations want a quick and straightforward way to understand what the nonprofit is all about. That is a key function of mission statements.

So how are strategies involved? Strategic planning often results in the identification of sustainability as a key value to the organization. For small or start up nonprofits, sustainability might take the form of hiring a paid executive director. For growing nonprofits, sustainability might look like grants to fund centrally important programs. For larger nonprofits, sustainability can be linked to capital campaigns to ensure required facilities and program space.

Strategic initiatives that focus on fundraising create impetus and grow into momentum to identify and establish revenue sources to support your organization's mission.

Stress Less Strategies Lift Employee Engagement

When organizations develop a strategic plan and the subsequent processes for measuring, evaluating and reframing strategic objectives, the mission and vision of the nonprofit becomes clearer in the eyes of the employees. Rather than a job or a paycheck, the employees come to work each day to be part of something meaningful. And when employees find their work meaningful, they become and stay engaged. And when employees are engaged, they take ownership of their work and become internally motivated (inspired) to create paths to success.

Take away the strategic plan and its relevant planning and evaluation processes, and the employee becomes a ship without an anchor or a windy sea, willing to jump to any ship in the vicinity that appears to be heading for more pleasant oceans.

Stress Less Strategies Add New Life to Workplace Doldrums

Similar to employee engagement, energy in the workplace becomes a continual cycle of growth and success. As a rule, human nature supplies sufficient energy to accomplish tasks that we deem of most value. The most tired teenager will still find sufficient energy to sit up in bed, grab the controller, and concentrate intensely on their favorite video game for hours. If your staff finds fulfillment in their work functions, they will devote their energies to fulfilling them. To help your employees find fulfillment, they must see work as meaningful to others and themselves. Strategic plans create the values, mission, vision and goals that provide meaning to the work your organization does. Then, the processes of

> To help your employees find fulfillment, they must see work as meaningful to others and themselves.

working as a team toward these goals, reviewing progress, measuring and evaluating results, and reappraising goals regularly creates in the employees a sense of purpose and collaboration to which they can feel satisfied in exchanging their precious energies and time.

Stress Less Strategies Encourage Employee and Leadership Accountability

Perhaps one of the most underappreciated results of the strategic planning process is the effect it has on leaders in the organization. Participating supervisors, managers, directors, executives and board members cannot help but grow in their leadership capabilities as they take on ownership of critical strategic initiatives and practice personal and professional accountability for the assignments they accept. Boards and executives should remember that accountability doesn't make perfect. Practice makes perfect. Developing employees into organizational leaders requires patience and support. When leaders make mistakes, a better question than, "how could you be so stupid?" would be, "what can we learn as leaders and as an organization from the experience?" I am not suggesting we overlook repeated careless mistakes. Rather than considering the results of a one-time blunder, we ought to discover he reasons behind the decisions to see if the developing leader requires additional training or our continued support.

Chapter Three: The Strategic Planning Session

Once you have a motivating reason to hold a strategic planning session and add the ongoing processes of strategic planning to your organization's culture, the following steps will help you plan for and run your first (or next) successful, stress less strategic planning session. The importance of first two decisions are easily overlooked by board members and the executive team. If you want a stress less strategic planning experience, do not overlook their importance.

Step 1: Location, Location, Location

What is true in real estate is true in strategic planning. The first BIG decision in planning and executing a successful, stress less strategic planning session is to find the right place to hold the session(s).

When it comes to the venue, the last place you want to be for a planning session is in your own office space. I don't care if you have mahogany accents throughout, the latest and most beautiful artwork, and a top-of-the-line A/V tech system in a spacious conference room. If you hold your session in your own office space, the routine that surrounds you will intrude upon your activities and, more critically, upon the creative mindset required for your participants. If they are one room or one hallway away from their computer, they will be constantly thinking of all the work they could be doing rather than sitting in "another meeting."

The same goes for the conference rooms of other participants invited to the planning session(s).

Consider the idea that the more unfamiliar and the less routine the space is for the participants, the more they can open their minds to possibilities not connected to their current, day-to-day realities.

Some organizations balk at the idea of flying their board and session participants to an exotic resort for a weekend strategic retreat. I used to think the same thing when I first started attending the annual conferences of a nonprofit industry I have been involved in. Some trade associations tend to hold their winter meetings at upscale destination resorts in Orlando, New Orleans, Las Vegas, San Diego and San Antonio. I initially saw a disconnect from the related travel and lodging expenses of attending such meetings. I thought, "if we are a nonprofit industry, why are we staying at lavish hotels for our meetings?" I was stuck in my little picture world, and I was not alone. I remember sharing an airport shuttle (long before Uber and Lyft came on the scene) from the airport to the resort with an attorney her own annual conference. She was staying at a decent hotel and was flabbergasted that our nonprofit association was holding our sessions at a fancier one.

Once explained to me, though, the reasoning was simple: if we held the session at the most affordable motel breakfast nook in Podunkville, few speakers would ever agree to attend. As it was, the association was able to bring in top representatives from various government agencies central to our association members' work. It was a lot easier to get a speaker (who cannot accept payment for attending) to agree to come to Orlando for a couple of days in January than to Podunkville in any season.

The same holds true for your strategic planning session. There will be some participants who will come no matter what: your executive team, your key staff leaders and employee representatives, and even most of your board. But to land the important stakeholders who do not feel obligated to attend (more below in step 3), sweetening the pot by holding it somewhere more exotic than your boardroom will absolutely make a difference. If you live near the coast, taking a two or three day cruise might even be a consideration (so long as the participating stakeholders have no trouble finding their sea legs).

"That's all fine and well for a large nonprofit or association with deep pockets," you say, "but what about my organization? Such a retreat would bankruptcy us." I recognize that few nonprofit organizations can afford to hold their planning sessions at a destination resort. The next recommendation, then, would be a resort within driving distance (1 to 2 hours). Most nonprofits can find a resort within a couple of hours where they might hold their critical planning meetings. Not only will the venue boost creativity, but your participants will actually look forward to the sessions rather than dreading them on the calendar.

Finally, I have worked with start ups and small coalitions who absolutely could not afford such destination resorts or even a local hotel board room. In such cases, your local library may have a nice meeting room you can schedule for free.

Step 2: Choose an Independent, Experienced and Unbiased Facilitator

You may have the most amazing public speaker in your organization (it may even be you). He or she may have experience facilitating meetings in the community and even in your own organization. He or she may be an expert at creating activities designed to promote the greatest amount of participation possible. He or she may even be a professional at managing contrasting personalities.

Regardless of his or her experience and expertise, the fact that he or she works for you and at your organization means that facilitating a meeting in an unbiased fashion is not possible. Using a subordinate to facilitate your meeting will inevitably mean that the contributions and opinions of the executives, the board, and the facilitator's direct boss will receive greater weight and respect than the contributions and opinions of the rest of the group. As much as you hope to save money, every in-house facilitator is, to some extent, a Yes-Man or Yes-Woman.

Using a third-party may not cost you an arm and a leg. Your top-of-the-line, 20+ year experienced facilitator could cost you several thousand dollars per day of facilitation. However, this will also include a great deal of consulting ahead of the session and a polished, practical follow up report, support by phone and email and, perhaps, in person if he or she is local.

Other professional facilitators may bill hourly, per package deal, or by day. Four hour sessions might run from a couple hundred dollars to a thousand or more. Such facilitators are likely to provide a more than satisfactory service that you will not regret.

If you are looking for free facilitators, consider your friends and those within your professional network who may have facilitated community panels, their own employee focus group, or other meetings with multiple participants of varied backgrounds. Be generous with them, though. Real facilitation requires hours of work in advance of the meeting, several hours of intense focus during the meeting, and hours of follow up to write, assemble, format, deliver and review a practical strategic planning report.

Step 3: Inviting the Right Stakeholders

All too often, nonprofit boards convene a strategic planning session with, of course, the executive director. They spend a day or two determining the direction they want to see the organization take, hashing out plans for the coming few years. They congratulate themselves at the end of the day, formalize the decisions made during the sessions, and hand them to the director asking him or her to "make it so" (yes, that is a Jean Luc Picard quote).

Obviously, from an outsider's perspective, such an approach to strategic planning will encounter resistance from multiple directions. When decisions are made by a small inner circle and those decisions affect the executive team, the management team, the employees, the clients, the vendors, and, in deed, the entire community, you can be sure that there will be virtually no buy in from any group except the inner circle. The dictatorial management style served Walt Disney and Steve Jobs well, but you have to ask yourself, "are you a Steve Jobs or a Walt Disney?"

Planning sessions must include representatives from all groups that have a role in achieving the meeting objectives and that will be affected by the meetings potential decisions. Referred to above, you should consider inviting to your strategic planning sessions your board and executive team, of course. Additionally, you department heads, key managers, aspiring and well-respected managers, high performing and connected employees, clients or customers who have provided constructive feedback in the past, key vendors, regulators, funders, and even representatives of the communities you serve.

How many is too many? While not a hard and fast rule, keeping a close balance between the board, executive team and directors/managers on one side and the employees, clients, vendors, regulators, funders and community representatives on the other side. If you have a massive board that already includes representatives from your funders, communities and vendors, then your invitation list may not extend too far beyond the board itself.

Personally, I prefer to work with groups of between 10 and 30 participants. Other meeting leaders might enjoy working with groups of 50. I find, though, that my activity-based style works best with groups of 30 or less. For larger groups (or for those under 10), I adapt my approach and still enjoy the experience, but I have identified my key customer size.

When considering whom to invite from each of these constituencies, do not ask who would be most likely to go along with our decisions. Rather, ask who is most likely to have real insight based upon experience and how likely are they to share that insight and their ideas in a respectful and constructive way. Avoid cherry picking favorites based upon how long you have known someone or whether you have family BBQs with them in the summer. In fact, the closer you are to them, the less likely they are to open up and share conflicting ideas that are critical to the strategic planning processes.

You might fear that your invitees will say, "no" to your invitation. After all, if they are not employees, why would the even consider spending a or two day with your team in planning sessions. Reasons will vary, but you will be surprised at who will accept and who will not. They may see it as a chance to help an organization they believe in. They may participate because of the chance to connect and network with others in the room. Many will participate solely on the opportunity to get away from their day-to-day work, especially if the venue is appealing to them (see Location, Location, Location above).

Once you have created the invitation list, make sure to get the invitations out plenty early so the potential participants can get the event on their schedule. It might be appropriate to send paper or electronic invitations to members of the board and those who receive a paycheck from the organization. However, the rest should be contacted personally, by phone or, when possible, in person. "Hey, can I stop by for a 10-minute visit next week? I have a proposition I would like to discuss with you in person." You can use the same technique via email to set up a phone meeting for those who do not live locally.

Finally, get input from your board and team. Do not assume that because you know who the top performing front line employee it that he or she should be the employee representative at the planning meeting. Ask your department heads and managers about the potential personality fit. If the employee is a team player, then absolutely consider inviting them. If he or she is a top performer because they sequester themselves, have no contact with other employees and or, conversely, are part of the gossip mill, you will want to avoid them like the plague.

Getting a mix of constituent representation at your planning meeting is critical to its success. Having a bunch of Yes Men and Yes Women will stifle creativity. You want imaginative input. You want respectful disagreement. You want energetic involvement. With such participants, your session will be not only productive but surprisingly enjoyable.

Step 4: Setting the Date

Here are a couple lessons I have learned about the importance of timing when it comes to scheduling meetings:

First, do not schedule meetings on weekends. Weekends are for time off, spending time with family, having fun, getting things down around the house, and even going to church. They are not for sitting in a room with strangers or business associates working on a topic that could be addressed during the week. People are more likely to justify taking off work on a weekday and attend a meeting of interest than they are to attend on a weekend.

Second, do not hold business meetings at night. People are no more likely to attend in the evening than they are during "normal business hours." Like weekends, evenings are for unwinding, hanging at home, or having fun on the town, not for sitting in a meeting.

When you begin considering the date, the schedule and the length of your next planning meeting, these are important rules to keep in mind. First of all, even if you don't have the venue or the agenda set, share a "Save the Date" invitation with your stakeholders, ideally six to twelve months out. If you are holding the meeting during the summer time or, and I do not recommend this, during spring break or holiday breaks, twelve months is preferable. If you choose a date when most people are usually on vacation, your invitees will be less likely to accept (or they will attend with a chip on their shoulder).

Some new or small organizations feel like they are intruding on their board's or stakeholders' professional lives by holding a meeting on a week day. I have led successful strategic planning meetings on Saturdays, but I do not recommend it. Ask yourself this question, "Would I rather someone intrude upon my professional life or upon my personal life?" I'm pretty sure the answer is professional life for most people.

So, schedule your meeting well in advance, and schedule it to take place during the work week.

If your stakeholders have children in school, consider consulting the local school district's calendar to make sure you are not scheduling during time off. Times during the year to avoid include within a week of all holidays, the days leading up to or following Super Bowl Sunday, spring break, the first half of June, and back-to-school time in August.

Finally, avoid holidays and vacation time. The exception to this rule would be destination retreats. If you are planning to hold your meeting (and reimburse all or a portion of your participants' travel and lodging), then holidays and school breaks might be great times to schedule your meetings. Your stakeholders will likely bring their spouse or partner and maybe even their family along. In such cases, keeping your meetings to half-days will be critical to holding your participants' attention.

Step 5: Creating the Agendas

How long should you plan to meet? Two hours? Four hours? Eight hours? More? Would it be better to hold the meeting on just one day or spread over two or three days?

I wish the answers to these questions were easier. They are not, but here are some guidelines to help:

One- and two-hour sessions are virtually useless. Unless you are holding such meetings monthly and getting regular attendance from all of your stakeholders, such short meetings will spend the first 30 minutes just getting reacquainted with the issues. Only hold one- to two-hour planning sessions if they are planned every month or two.

At this point, let's use an a la carte menu to figure out how many hours you will need to plan on. The following suggestions are for meetings with up to twenty or so participants. If you plan to have 30 participants, add an addition 50% of time to the following recommendations. For 50 participants, double the recommended time.

Strategic Planning Session Objective	Expected Agenda Time
Create a Values Statement:	One Hour
Create a Mission Statement:	Two Hours
Create a three- to five-year Vision Statement:	Two hours
Develop Annual Objectives (2-4) tied to the Vision Statement:	One Hour per Objective
Establish Measurable Goals to meet the Annual Objectives:	Two hours per Annual Objective Hour
Determining Tactics for achieving each Goal and Assigning Accountability:	One hour per goal
Quarterly, semi-annual, or annual reviews of Statements, Objectives, Goals and Tactics:	One hour per item

    Organizations meeting for the first time in a strategic planning session will likely need a minimum of eight hours to address their Values, Mission, Vision, Objectives and Goals, though twelve hours over two or three consecutive days is pretty common. What would this look like, in scheduling terms? Perhaps your hold your first 4-hour session on Monday afternoon. Tuesday morning, you convene again for either an eight-hour session to be done in two days or a four-hour session to wrap up with the final four-hour session Wednesday morning.

    Evaluation meetings (follow ups) might make sense to hold in either one four-hour block or split between two days, depending upon how much needs to be reviewed, analyzed and reassigned.

    You will need two versions of the meeting agenda. The first is for the meeting leader. This includes each activity, its timeframe (estimated start and stop times), its purpose, the details the leader needs to facilitate the activity, any supplies and/or equipment required, and key questions and cues that will be helpful for managing the discussion.

    The second agenda is for the meeting participants themselves. This version is a simplified version of the meeting leader's agenda. It need only have the timeframe for the activities, a name for each activity, and when and how long the breaks are anticipated to be.

    The great news for those leaders working with a professional meeting facilitator is that your facilitator can provide invaluable guidance and input on such planning matters.

Step 6: Supplies & Equipment

You do not have to purchase half of the office supply store in anticipation of your planning session. A few simple supplies and copies of some basic handouts will suffice. Make sure that you have the right equipment (projector, computers, tablets, etc.) and supplies for the session far ahead of time. I recommend that you avoid the rigidity of PowerPoint presentations and their tendencies toward mind-numbing wordiness and lack of creativity.

Here is a list of the minimal supplies and equipment you should have with you in advance of the meeting:
- Various sizes and colors of sticky notes (3-5 different colors, from 2" to 6" in width)
- Permanent markers of various dark colors (at least one per participant)
- Large self-sticking poster sheets or easel paper
- Small red, yellow and green sticky flags
- Activity handouts for each participant
- Rules of Engagement for each participant
- Meeting leader agenda
- Participant agenda
- Pens, pencils and notepads
- Meeting evaluation sheet for each participant
- Camera or smartphone for photographing activities and resulting decisions (e.g. easel paper or posters with notes)

Step 7: The Set Up

You might dismiss this as someone else's responsibility, but the best planned meeting with the perfect agenda and the right participants will fail if you don't set up the room properly. Avoid at all costs theater-style and classroom-style seating arrangements. Planning meetings rely on face-to-face interactions, not shoulder-to-shoulder encounters. Large round tables can work, but even then, it is difficult to interact with someone opposite you or even hear what they are saying. Personally, I prefer either four people per round or square table (the size of a card table) or eight people per rectangular table (like a dinner table). There must be plenty of room between tables to be able to hear those at your own table. Consequently, avoid booking a room that would have your participants feeling like there can't lean their chair back without bumping into another participant. If you hold your meeting in a crowded room, your discussion will feel as cramped and stifled as your participants. Find a room with high ceilings (soaring would be great) and plenty of elbow room. Open rooms lead to open minds

Manage room windows carefully. If you are meeting in a mountain top or sea side hotel with wonderful views, keep the curtains drawn during brainstorming and creative-based activities. Close them when you need your team to focus on details.

Provide your participants with food. Snack breaks are a must ever two hours at minimum. Have small snacks and water available at all times at the tables. These snacks might include wrapped hard candies, mini-chocolates or Hershey kisses, individual bowls of nuts or pretzels (avoid community grab bags or bowls) or bags of popcorn. That said, do not provide too much sugar or too much salt throughout the day. Mix it up. Provide meals on site and give participants a chance to eat in the room with the curtains opened or on a patio or deck with a view. Do not make them got off site to get their own meal. You will lose precious meeting time and opportunities for critical casual interactions.

Finally, set up the meeting rules up front. Either pass out a handout with rules in large letters or post the rules on the front wall in writing large enough to be seen from every table. These rules should address

- Cell-phone usage: place on silent or vibrate and store out of sight except for emergency calls which are to be taken outside the room
- Respect for the opinions of others: avoid interrupting, dominating or belittling discussion points
- A "Parking Lot" space for ideas that are good but not relevant to the discussion: usually a large self-sticking poster sheet on the side wall
- The expectation of confidentiality for and from participants
- Housekeeping issues: where to find water, the restrooms, smoking areas, etc.

Chapter Four: Conclusion

The seven simple steps described in the previous chapter can help any organizational leaders be ready for an upcoming strategic planning session. Following these steps increases confidence in facilitating a positive outcome, thus decreasing the stress associated with the worry that such meetings will waste time and embarrass the leadership.

If stress results from the difference between expectations and reality, then preparing for a strategic planning session can easily become a major stress in the lives of the executive, board chair and anyone else involved. From the lack of clarity of the meeting objectives to the possible insecurity of planning a meeting that seems overwhelming in detail, to the frustration of trying to find the right professional consultant without breaking the budget, stress is ubiquitous throughout the process.

Following the steps above increases your clarity of purpose, minimizes the insecurity of leading a boring or poorly planned meeting, and eliminates the frustration related to preparing the numerous details for a strategic planning session. This means less stress. And if you have a business to run, people to manage, and a personal life to live, additional stress is the last thing you need.

Glossary

Board Meeting: A regular gathering of board members and executives held on a regular interval often defined in the organization's bylaws or policies. Board meetings should focus on high level issues, include major policies and critical problems. Board meetings should not get involved in tactics, though brief reports on critical goals and objectives can be appropriate.

External Document: A document whose target audience is outside of the organization, including clients, customers, vendors, regulators, funders and the general public.

Facilitator: The individual responsible for managing the meeting discussions and activities. Professional facilitators are experts in creating and leading activities that include all attendees and achieve objectives without allowing hierarchical or personal biases to dominate the direction of the meeting.

Goals: Measurable activities that, together with other goals, serve as reliable indicators that annual objectives are being met.

Internal Document: A document whose target audience is inside of the organization, including board members, executive leadership, department directors, management, employees, and even volunteers. Their purpose is to provide direction, inspiration and clarification with regards to the organization's core principles.

Leadership Retreat: A meeting (typically from a half-day to 2 days) of the executive team, board members, department directors and key managers with the purpose of developing leadership skills, evaluating and building upon strategic objectives, goals and tactics, or re-energizing participants through inspirational presentations.

Meeting Leader: See Facilitator

Mission Statement: A brief description (typically a few words to two sentences) of the organization's reason for being. A well-crafted mission statement is motivational, simple in its construction and easy for both clients and employees to remember. Organizational leadership uses the mission statements as a standard against which they can measure the appropriateness of all organizational activities, initiatives and programs

Objectives: Annual ambitions identified during strategic planning that allow the organization to evaluate progress and movement toward the organization's vision statement.
Stakeholders: Any individual with an interest in the mission or processes of the organization. Stakeholders might include employees and board members, but they also include clients and customers, vendors and funders, and even regulators, local politicians and community leaders.
Strategic Plan: A detailed report resulting from a strategic planning session or sessions that typically include the current organizational values, mission and vision statements along with annual objectives, identified goals, and critical tactics with assigned stakeholders to identify accountability.
Strategic Planning: An ongoing process he includes the strategic planning meeting, annual and quarterly evaluations, monthly leadership reports, weekly updates and even daily huddles. The strategic planning process should involves all stakeholders on a regular basis.
Strategic Planning Session: A gathering of stakeholders, typically for a half-day to 2 days, during which the participants create and/or reevaluate the organization's central strategic statements (Values, Mission, Vision). The longer sessions will also include the identification of annual objectives, measurable goals, tactics for approaching goals, and assignments to identify accountability. Strategic planning sessions should be held every one to five years.
Tactics: Specific plans for reaching strategic goals. Tactics are approaches and methods that stakeholders use as they work on goals for which they are accountable.
Values Statement: a list of typically 3 to 5 core principles (values) by which everything done in your organization can be judged to be "true to itself." This can be both an internal and an external document or jt an internal document.
Vision Statement: An internal document that provides guidance to organizational stakeholders, establishing milestones to achieve as an organization, typically in the coming three to five years.

Index

Goals, 16, 26
Mission Statement, 13, 15, 16, 26, 31
Objectives, 26
Strategic Plan, 11, 14, 15, 16
Strategic planning, 15, 17
Strategic planning report, 21
Strategic planning session, 11, 19, 20, 22, 26, 29, 32
Tactics, 11, 26, 32
Values Statement, 16, 26
Vision Statement, 16, 26

About the Author

Todd R. Christensen founded Todd R. Christensen Consulting in 2017 after seeing a need among the nonprofit and business communities he worked within for help with business meetings, strategic planning sessions and board meetings. With nearly 15 years of facilitating almost 2,000 workshops for a nationwide nonprofit agency, Todd also brings a master's degree in management with specializations in strategy and change management.

Todd consults with business and nonprofit leaders and facilitates planning sessions, board meetings, leadership development and other gatherings to avoid the embarrassment, aggravation and frustration of poorly planned or poorly led meetings.

Todd can be reached at Todd R. Christensen Consulting via www.ToddRChristensen.com, (208) 649-4788, Todd@ToddRChristensen.com or @trcconsultant.